© Copyright 2021 - All rights reserved.

You may not reproduce, duplicate or send the contents of this book without direct written permission from the author. You cannot hereby despite any circumstance blame the publisher or hold him or her to legal responsibility for any reparation, compensations, or monetary forfeiture owing to the information included herein, either in a direct or an indirect way.

Legal Notice: This book has copyright protection. You can use the book for personal purpose. You should not sell, use, alter, distribute, quote, take excerpts or paraphrase in part or whole the material contained in this book without obtaining the permission of the author first.

Disclaimer Notice: You must take note that the information in this document is for casual reading and entertainment purposes only. We have made every attempt to provide accurate, up to date and reliable information. We do not express or imply guarantees of any kind. The persons who read admit that the writer is not occupied in giving legal, financial, medical or other advice. We put this book content by sourcing various places.

Please consult a licensed professional before you try any techniques shown in this book. By going through this document, the book lover comes to an agreement that under no situation is the author accountable for any forfeiture, direct or indirect, which they may incur because of the use of material contained in this document, including, but not limited to errors, omissions, or inaccuracies.

Sight Words Activity Workbook

This workbook belongs to

SIGHT WORD PRACTICE

LET'S HAVE FUN TOGETHER WHILE LEARNING AND PRACTICING
SIGHT WORDS IN A VERY EASY AND FUNNY WAY.

> LEARN TO READ, WRITE, SPELL AND BUILD VOCABULARY WITH BELLOW FREQUENTLY USED SIGHT WORDS:

Practice learning to read and write with bellow most Common Sight Word

Fun and playful illustrations to build engagement, Hidden Sight words activity

Materials are organized with progressive skill building, to boost your kid's comprehension!

Quick Letter Tracing Reminder
Capital Alphabet
Trace all the Capital Letters

A B C D
E F G H
I J K L
M N O P
Q R S T
U V W X
Y Z

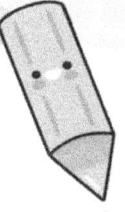

Small Alphabet
Trace all the small Letters

a b c d

e f g h

i j k l

m n o p

q r s t

u v w x

y z

Capital Alphabet
Dot to dot
Join all the Alphabet from A to Z

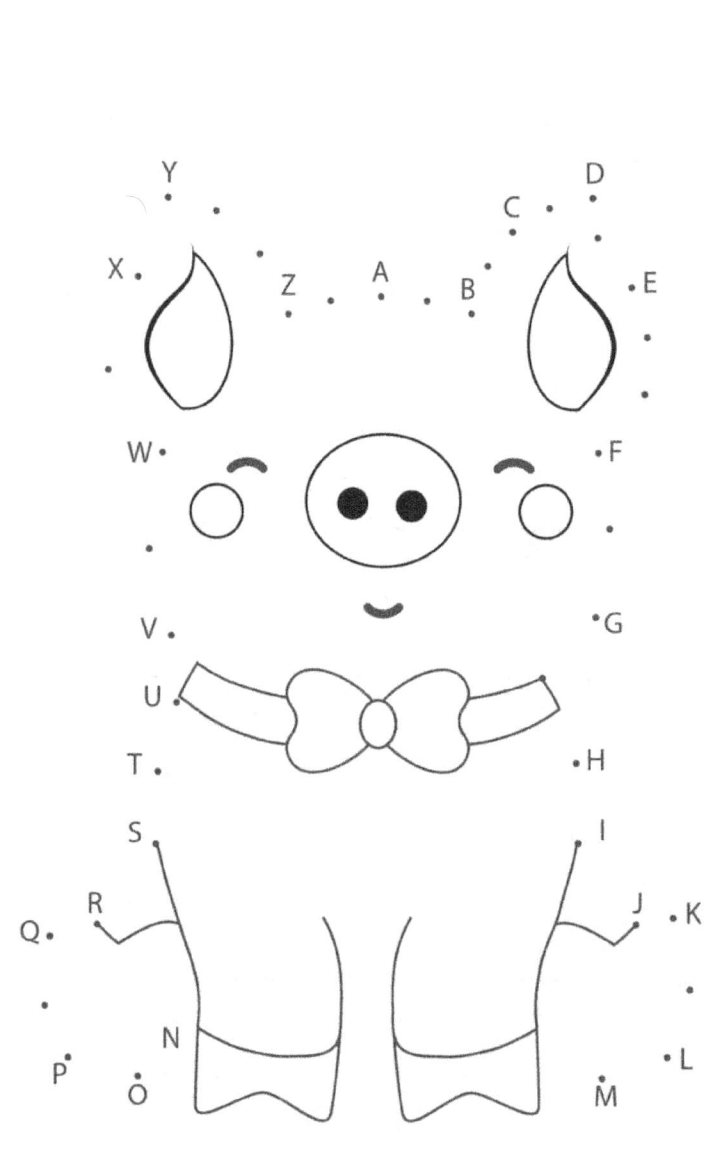

Small Alphabet Dot to dot

Join all the Alphabet from a to z

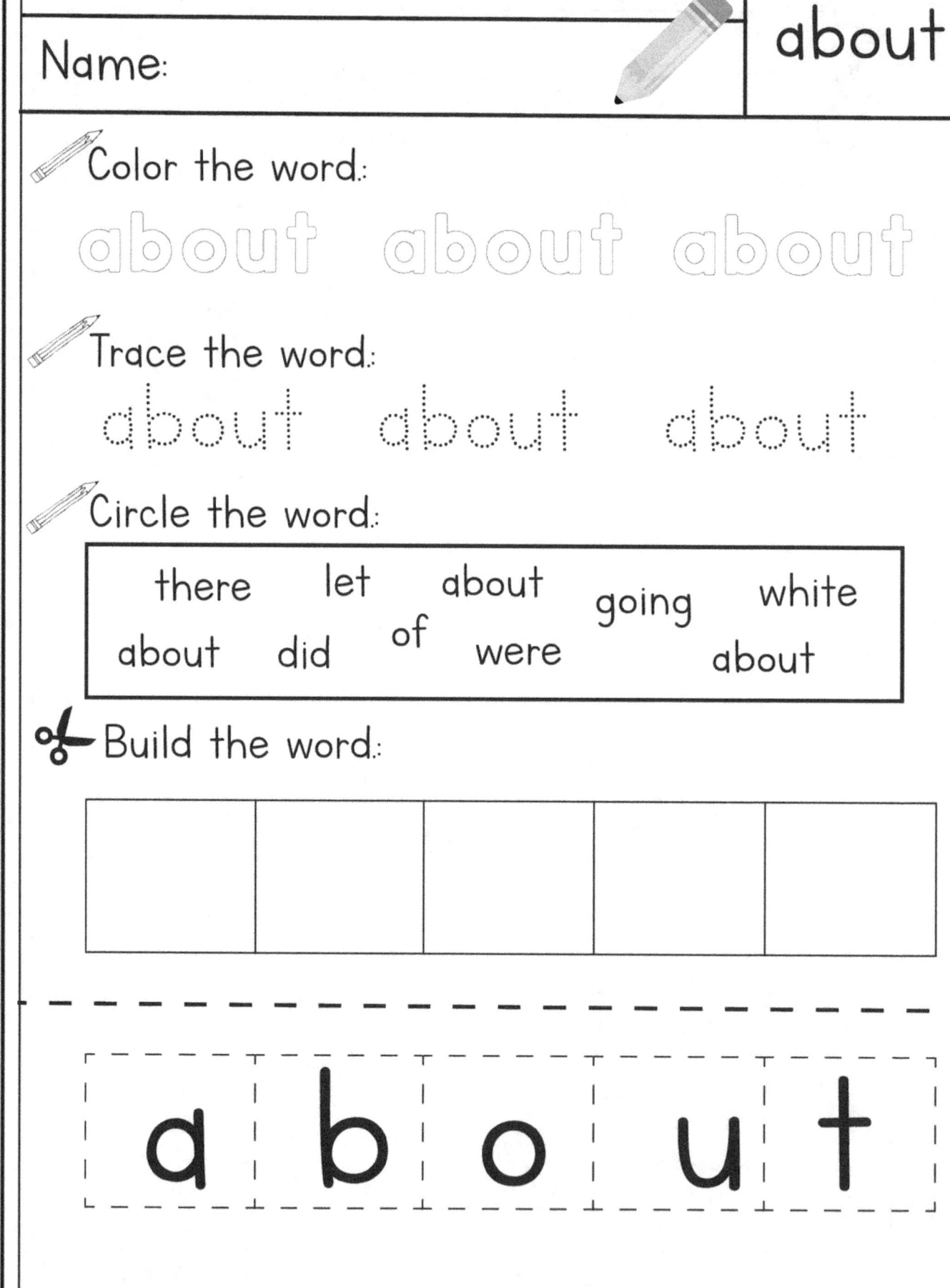

Name: | better

✏️ Color the word:

better better better

✏️ Trace the word:

better better better

✏️ Circle the word:

| better | better | pretty | came | white |
| pretty | came | white | better | pretty |

✂️ Build the word: ✂️

- -

| b | e | t | t | e | r |

Name: _____ | bring

✏️ Color the word:

bring   bring   bring

✏️ Trace the word:

bring   bring   bring

✏️ Circle the word:

there	let	bring		going	white
bring	did	of	were		bring

✂️ Build the word:

- -

| b | r | i | n | g |

Name: _____

carry

✏️ Color the word:

carry carry carry

✏️ Trace the word:

carry   carry   carry

✏️ Circle the word:

| there | let | carry | going | white |
| carry | did | of | were | carry |

✂️ Build the word:

- -

| c | a | r | r | y |

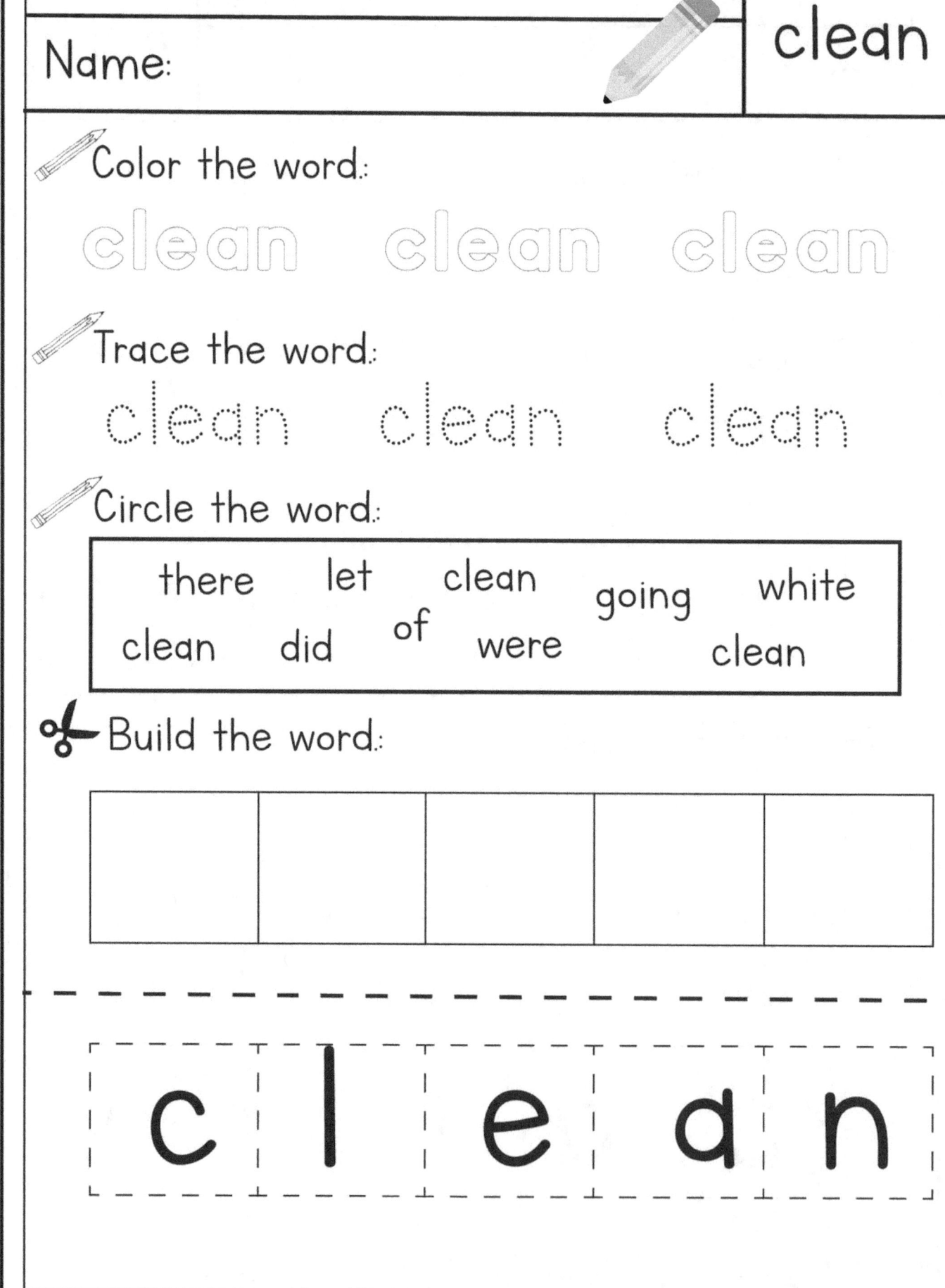

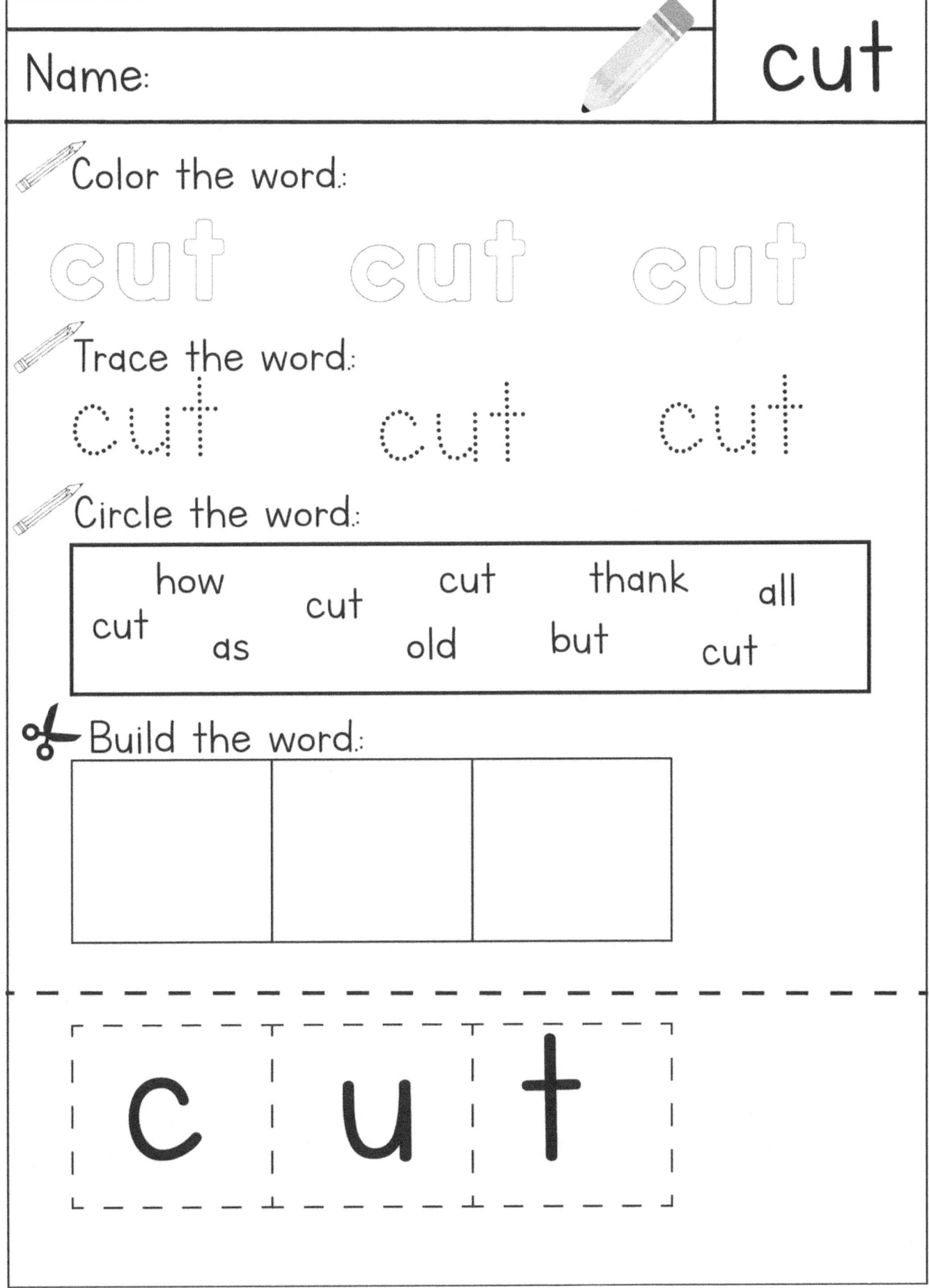

Name: | done

✏️ Color the word:

done done done

✏️ Trace the word:

done done done

✏️ Circle the word:

| get | put | have | done | she |
| walk | done | stop | let | have |

✂️ Build the word:

| | | | |

- - - - - - - - - -

| d | o | n | e |

Name: | draw

Color the word:

draw   draw   draw

Trace the word:

draw   draw   draw

Circle the word:

| get | put | have | draw | she |
| walk | draw | stop | let | have |

Build the word:

| | | | |

d | r | a | w

Name: _____ | drink

✏️ Color the word:

drink   drink   drink

✏️ Trace the word:

drink   drink   drink

✏️ Circle the word:

| there | let | drink | going | white |
| drink | did | of | were | drink |

✂️ Build the word:

- -

| d | r | i | n | k |

Name:

eight

✏️ Color the word:

eight   eight   eight

✏️ Trace the word:

eight   eight   eight

✏️ Circle the word:

| there | let | eight | going | white |
| eight | did | of | were | eight |

✂️ Build the word:

- -

| e | i | g | h | t |

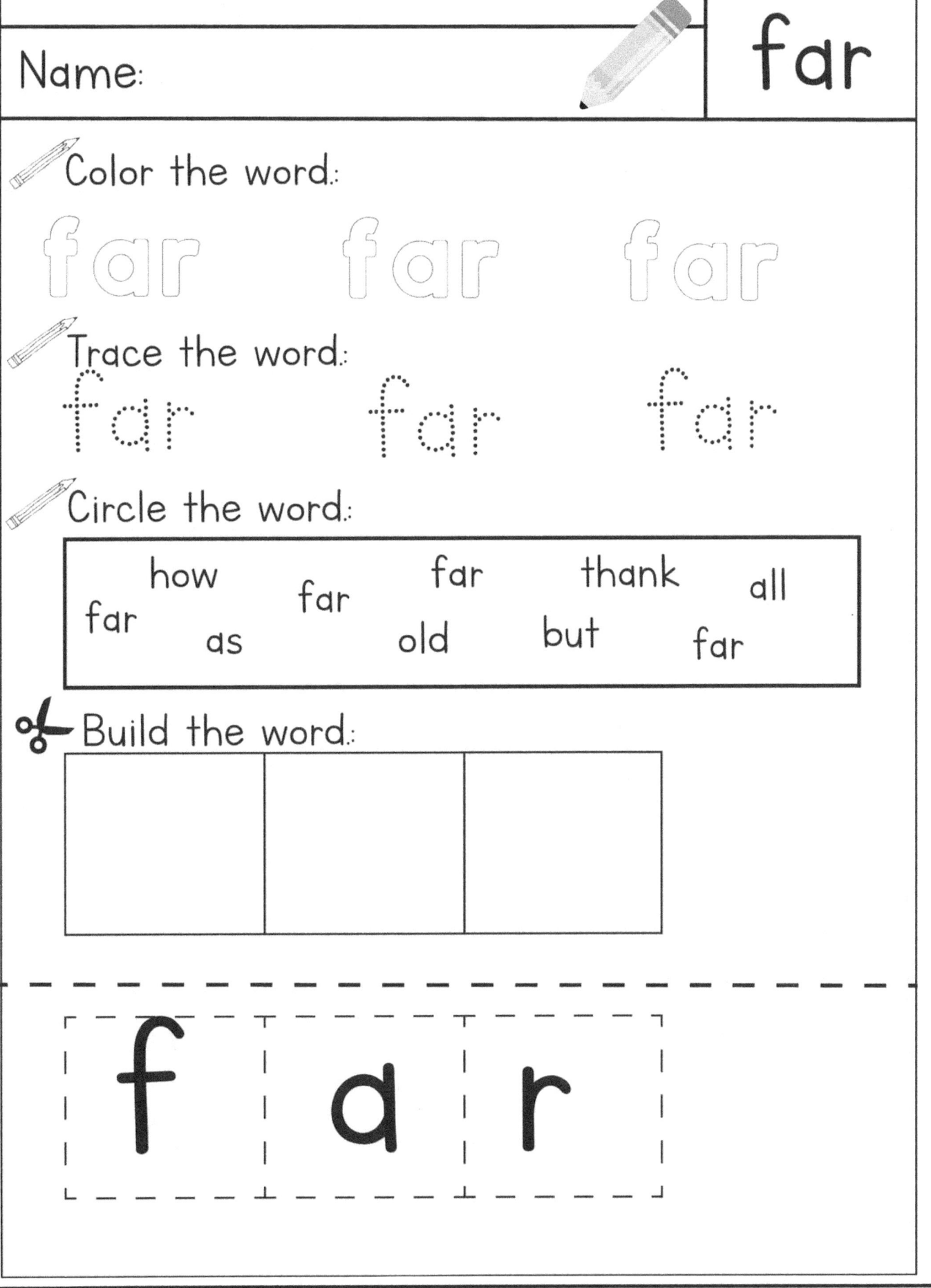

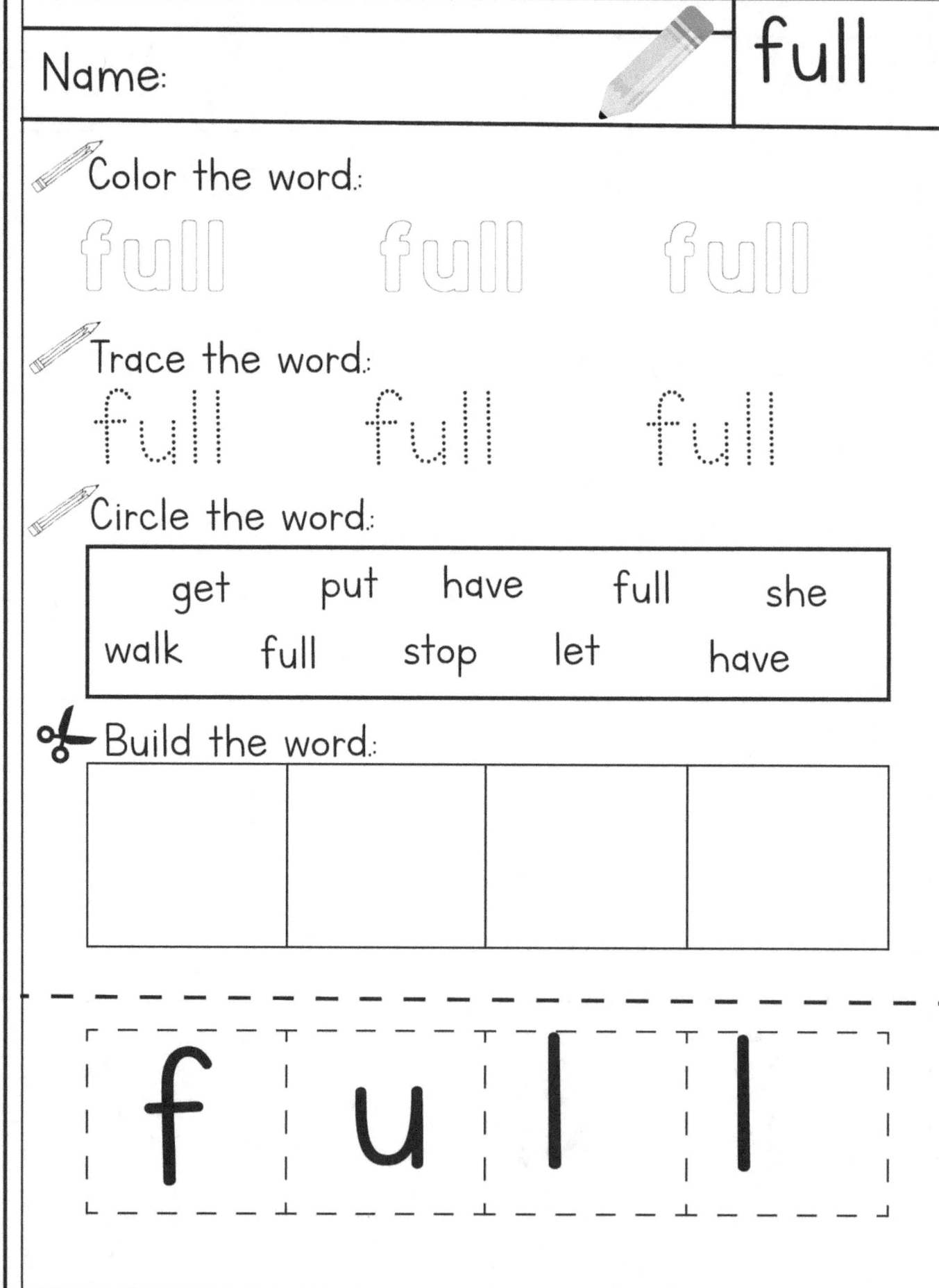

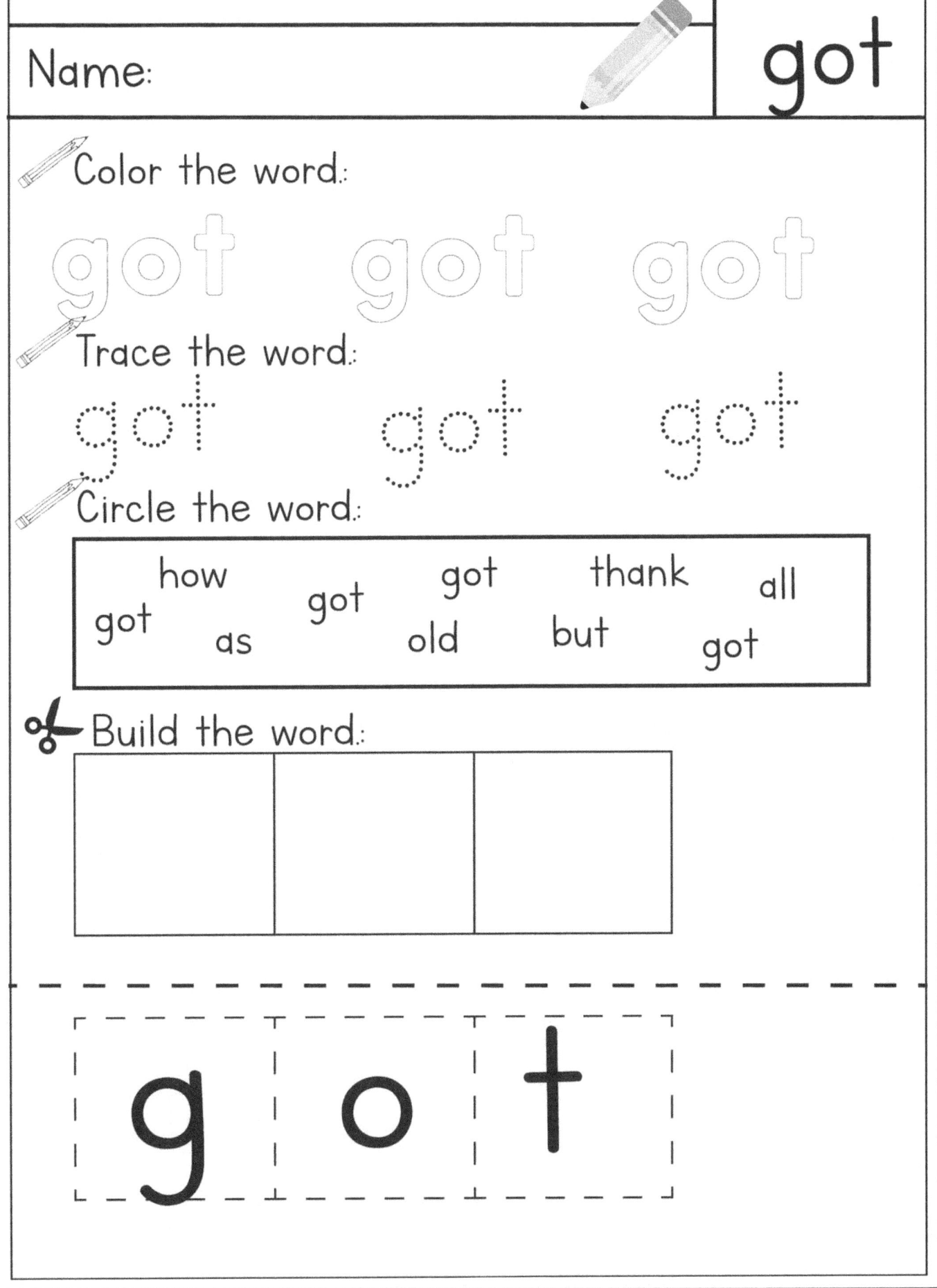

Name: _____ grow

Color the word:

grow grow grow

Trace the word:

grow   grow   grow

Circle the word:

get   put   have   grow   she
walk   grow   stop   let   have

Build the word:

- -

g | r | o | w

Name: _____

hold

✏️ Color the word:

hold   hold   hold

✏️ Trace the word:

hold   hold   hold

✏️ Circle the word:

| get | put | have | hold | she |
| walk | hold | stop | let | have |

✂️ Build the word:

- -

| h | o | l | d |

Name:

hurt

✏️ Color the word:

hurt   hurt   hurt

✏️ Trace the word:

hurt   hurt   hurt

✏️ Circle the word:

| get | put | have | hurt | she |
| walk | hurt | stop | let | have |

✂️ Build the word:

- -

| h | u | r | t |

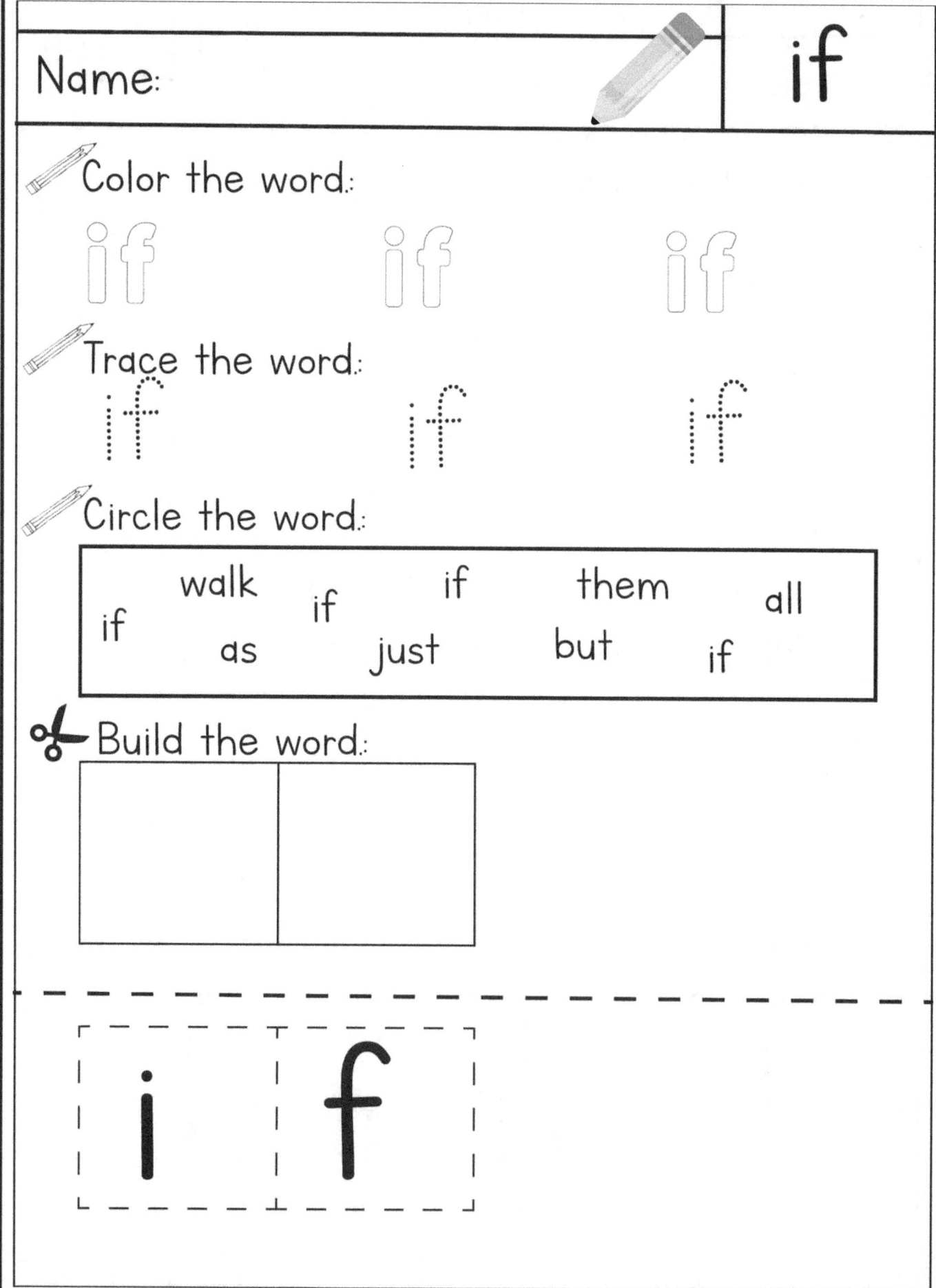

Name:

kind

Color the word:

kind kind kind

Trace the word:

kind kind kind

Circle the word:

get   put   have   kind   she
walk   kind   stop   let   have

Build the word:

k | i | n | d

Name: _____ | laugh

✏️ Color the word:

laugh   laugh   laugh

✏️ Trace the word:

laugh   laugh   laugh

✏️ Circle the word:

| there | let | laugh | going | white |
| laugh | did | of | were | laugh |

✂️ Build the word:

- -

| l | a | u | g | h |

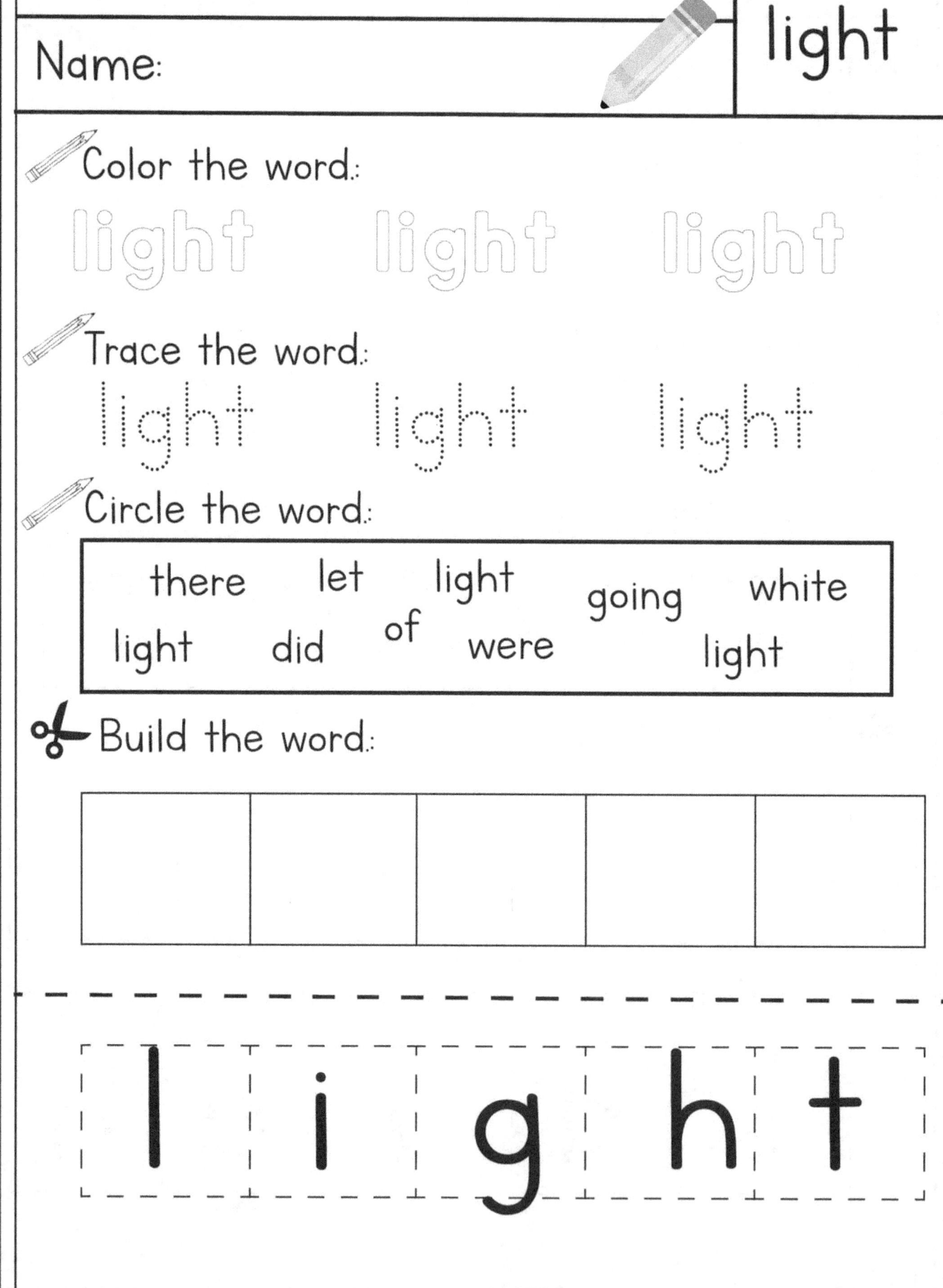

Name: _____ | long

✏️ Color the word:

long   long   long

✏️ Trace the word:

long   long   long

✏️ Circle the word:

| get | put | have | long | she |
| walk | long | stop | let | have |

✂️ Build the word:

- - - - - - - - - - - - - - - - - - - -

| l | o | n | g |

Name: | much

Color the word:

much much much

Trace the word:

much much much

Circle the word:

get   put   have   much   she
walk   much   stop   let   have

Build the word:

- - - - - - - - - - - - - - - - - -

| m | u | c | h |

Name: _____ | myself

✏️ Color the word:

myself myself myself

✏️ Trace the word:

myself myself myself

✏️ Circle the word:

myself myself pretty   came   white
pretty came   white   myself   pretty

✂️ Build the word:

- - - - - - - - - - - - - - - - - - - -

| m | y | s | e | l | f |

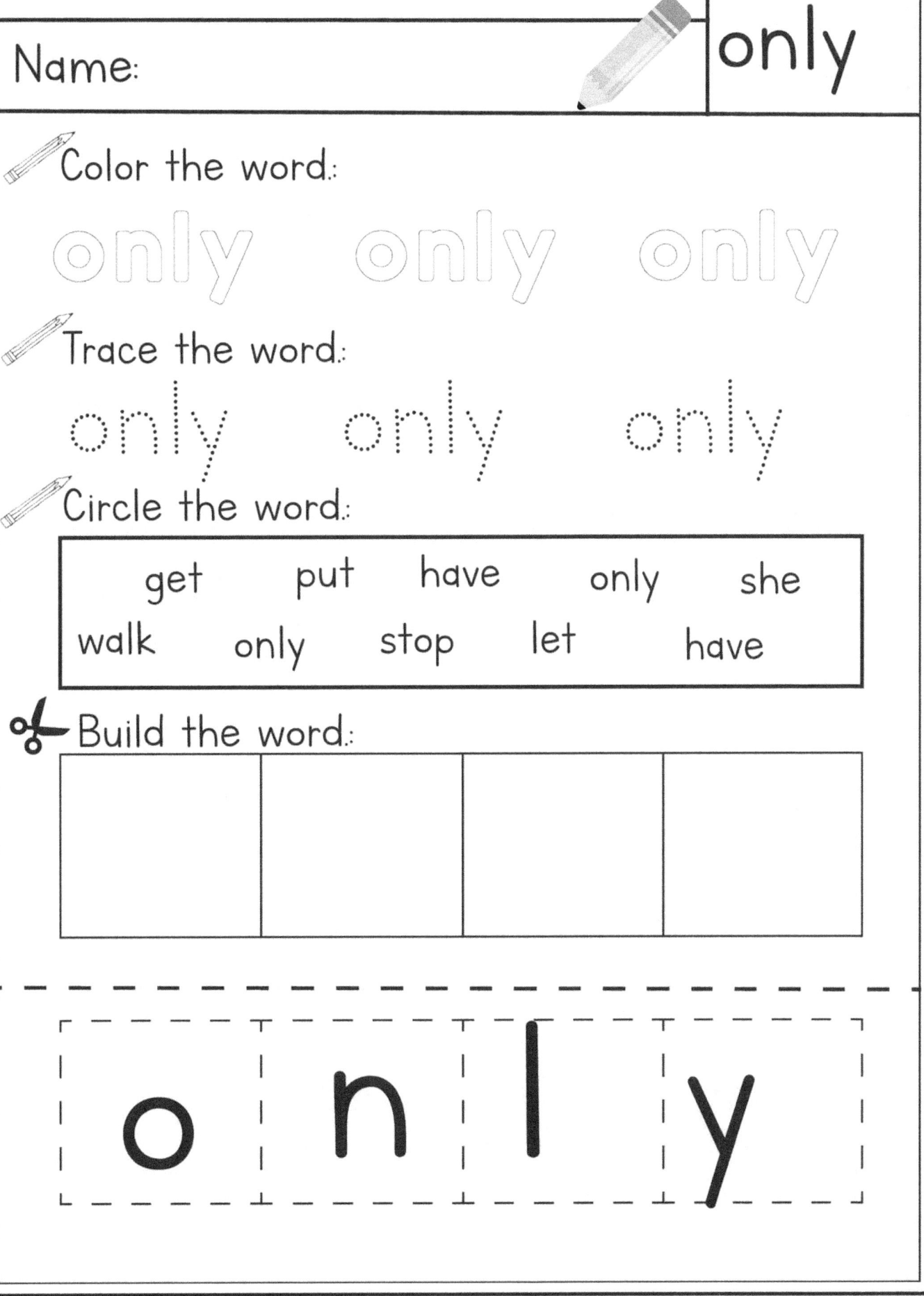

Name: **own**

✏️ Color the word:

own   own   own

✏️ Trace the word:

own   own   own

✏️ Circle the word:

how   own   thank   all
own   own
   as   old   but   own

✂️ Build the word:

- - - - - - - - - - - - - - - -

o | w | n

Name: | seven

Color the word:

seven seven seven

Trace the word:

seven seven seven

Circle the word:

| there | let | seven | going | white |
| seven | did | of | were | seven |

Build the word:

s e v e n

Name: _____ | shall

✏ Color the word:

shall   shall   shall

✏ Trace the word:

shall   shall   shall

✏ Circle the word:

| there | let | shall | going | white |
| shall | did | of | were | shall |

✂ Build the word:

- -

| s | h | a | l | l |

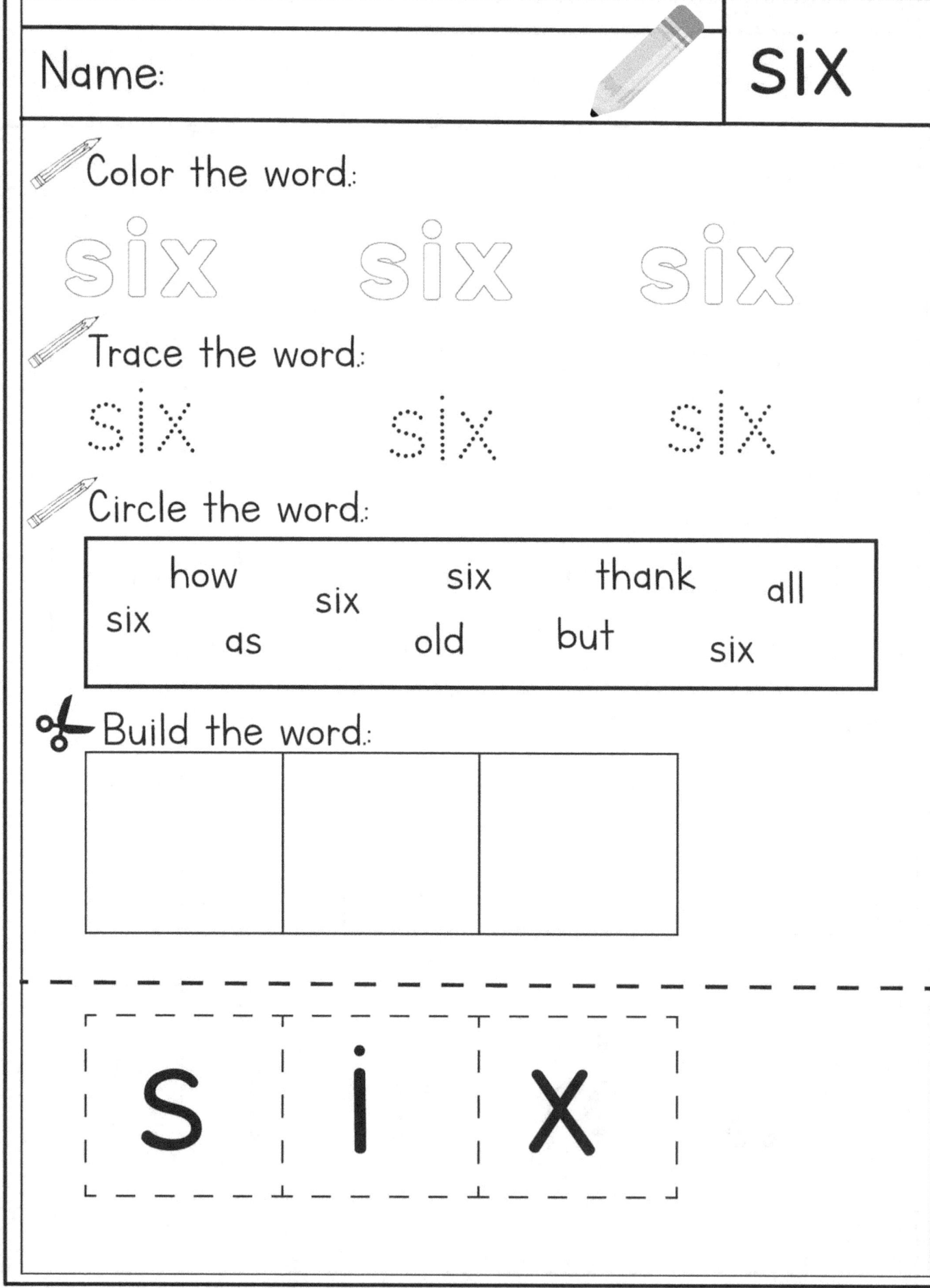

Name: _____ | show

✏️ Color the word:

show show show

✏️ Trace the word:

show   show   show

✏️ Circle the word:

| get | put | have | show | she |
| walk | show | stop | let | have |

✂️ Build the word:

- -

| s | h | o | w |

Name:

small

✏️ Color the word:

small   small   small

✏️ Trace the word:

small   small   small

✏️ Circle the word:

| there | let | small | going | white |
| small | did | of | were | small |

✂️ Build the word:

- -

| s | m | a | l | l |

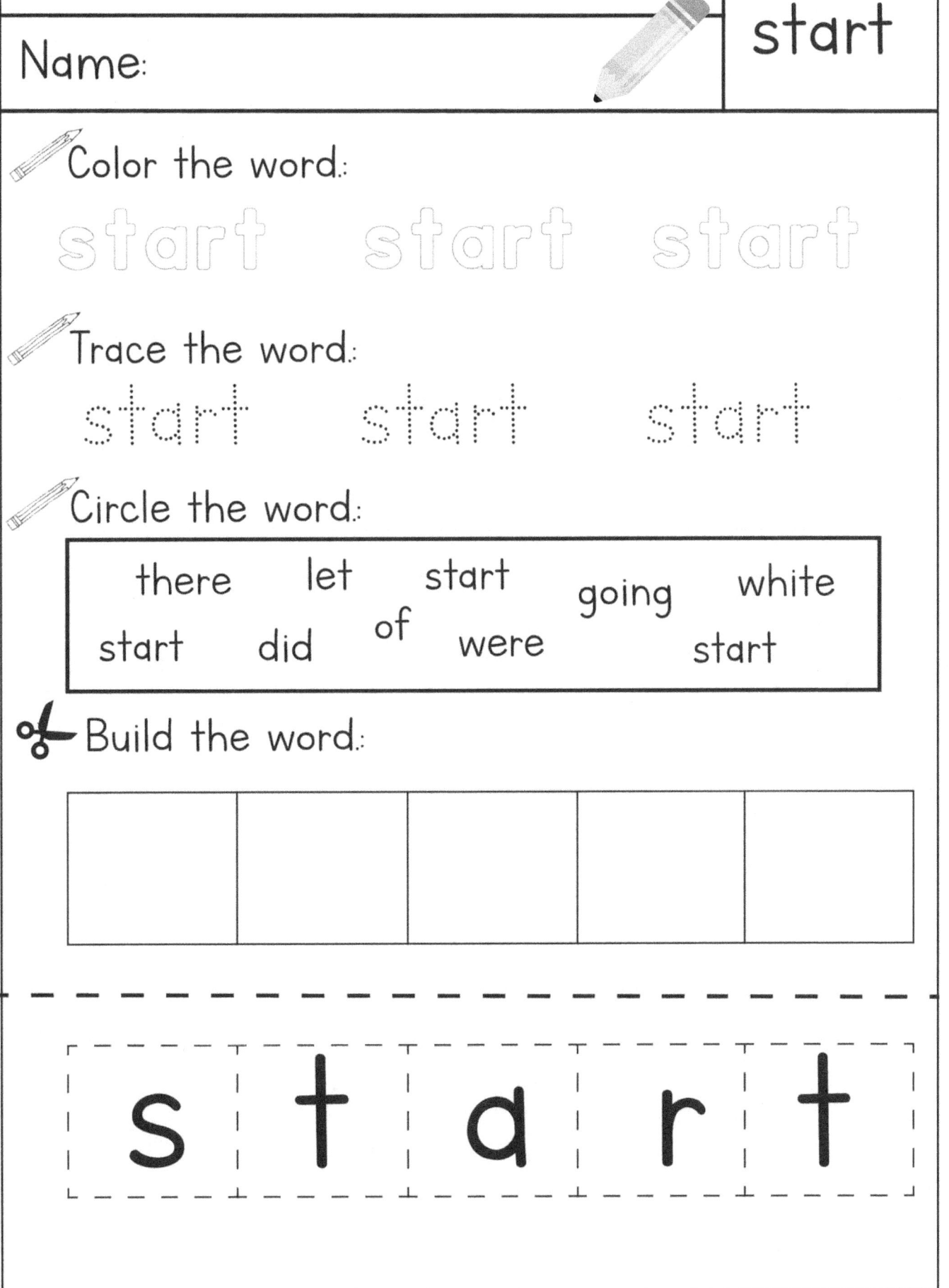

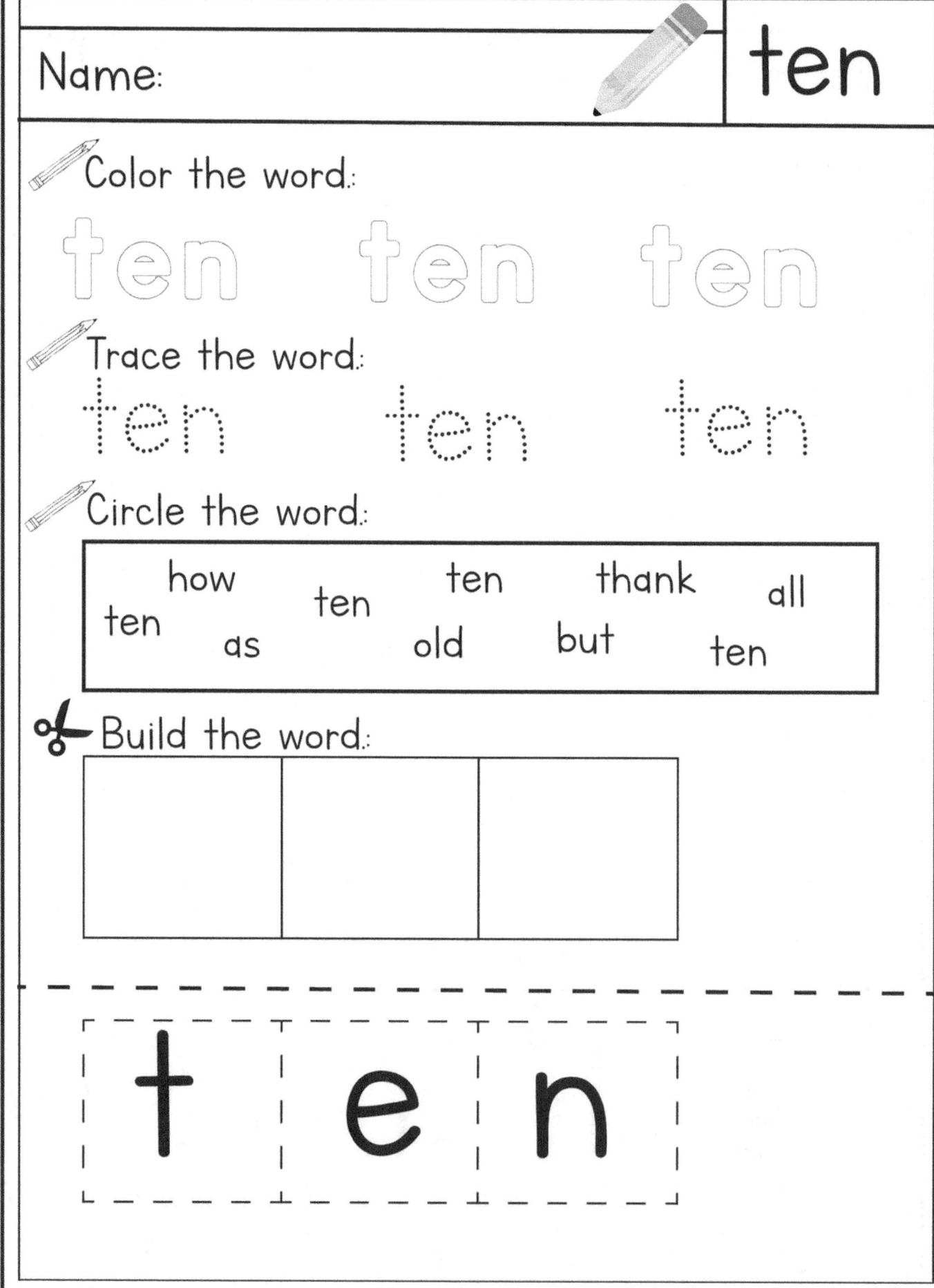

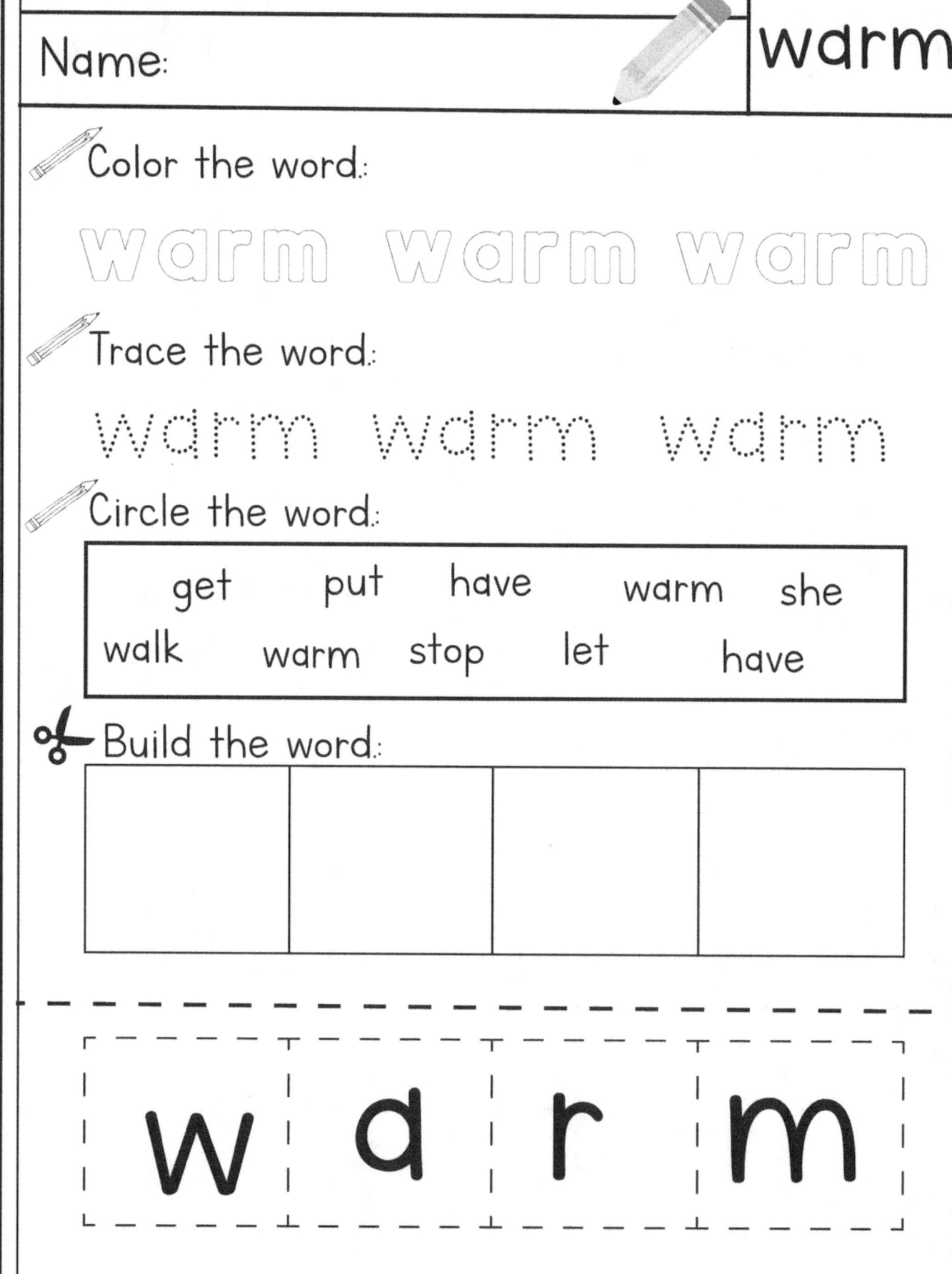

Tracing

Sight Words

 TRACE THE WORDS & PRACTICE WRITING

Alice Alice

apple apple

Ben Ben Ben

ball ball ball

Charlie Charlie

carrot carrot

Tracing — ABC Sight Words

 TRACE THE WORDS & PRACTICE WRITING

Daisy Daisy

dog dog dog

Emily Emily

egg egg egg

Franklin Franklin

frog frog

Tracing

ABC Sight Words

✏️ TRACE THE WORDS & PRACTICE WRITING

Grace Grace

giraffe giraffe

Henry Henry

hat hat hat

Isabel Isabel

ice cream

Tracing

Sight Words

 TRACE THE WORDS & PRACTICE WRITING

Jack Jack

jeep jeep jeep

Kate Kate

kite kite kite

Lucas Lucas

lion lion lion

Tracing

ABC Sight Words

✏️ **TRACE THE WORDS & PRACTICE WRITING**

Monica Monica

mouse mouse

Nicole Nicole

net net net

Oscar Oscar

owl owl owl

Tracing

 TRACE THE WORDS & PRACTICE WRITING

Peter Peter

parrot parro

Quentin

quilt quilt quilt

Rosie Rosie

rabbit rabbit

Tracing

ABC Sight Words

✏️ TRACE THE WORDS & PRACTICE WRITING

Sofia Sofia

sun sun sun

Thomas Ben

tiger tiger

Uriel Uriel Uriel

Umbrella

Tracing

A B C

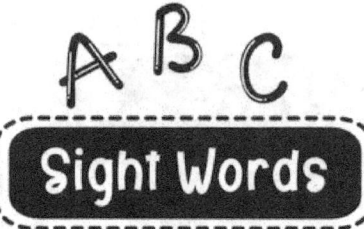

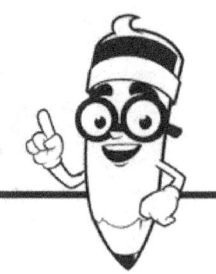

Sight Words

TRACE THE WORDS & PRACTICE WRITING

Victoria

violin violin

Wendy Wendy

wolf wolf

Xavier Xavier

x-ray x-ray

Tracing — Sight Words

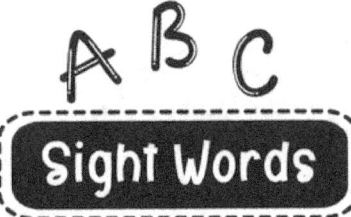

✏️ **TRACE THE WORDS & PRACTICE WRITING**

Yara Yara

yoga yoga

Zeke Zeke

zebra zebra

Tracing

✏️ **PRACTICE WRITING**

Tracing

✏️ **PRACTICE WRITING**

Tracing

✏️ **PRACTICE WRITING**

Reading and Writing
read the story and answer the questions below

PLAYFUL HIPPO

I can see a Hippo.
He is playful.
He is Happy.
The Hippo likes to play.

1) I can see a _____
   a) hippo   a) lion

2) He is _____
   a) sad   a) happy

3) The hippo likes to _____
   a) play   a) sing

Prepositions

Match the picture with the correct preposition

out

on

under

behind

above

in

Rhyming words
Circle the correct Rhyming word from the list

bag

tag   cot   try

bed

how   led   sat

pot

mop   sat   hot

van

sat   can   man

Rhyming words
Circle the correct Rhyming word from the list

sun

top   hat   fun

pin

cat   tin   sat

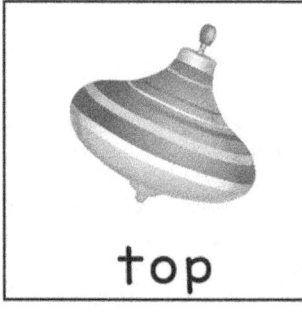
top

mop   sat   fun

dog

man   fur   fog

Sight words

Find the hidden Sightwords from the picture
and write them down

Sight words

_____ _____ _____ _____

_____ _____ _____ _____

Sight words

Find the hidden Sightwords from the picture and write them down

Hidden words in picture: up, and, said, the, can, is

Sight words

_____   _____   _____   _____

_____   _____   _____   _____

Missing Beginning and Ending letters

Find and fill the missing letter from the given combination below

| m | e | k | f | w | b |

__ey

ja__

nos__

__ox

__rog

__eb

Missing Beginning and Ending letters

Find and fill the missing letter from the given combination below

| x | p | b | e | t | p |

__ed

fo __

mo __

__ap

__an

be __

Vowels

write down the correct vowel and
re-write the word below

 __pple

 d__g

 b__ll

 c__p

 s__t

 s__d

Vowels

write down the correct vowel sounds

a e i o u

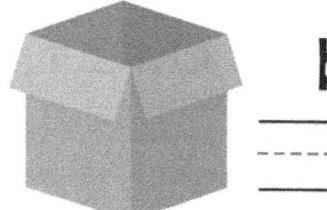 b __ x

 __ gg

 b __ n

 c __ t

 t __ p

 s __ n

Phonics Phase 2
s, a, t, p

match the picture with the correct phonic

strawberry

ant

teddy

pig

. a

. t

. s

. p

Phonics Phase 2
g, o, c, k
match the picture with
the correct phonic

  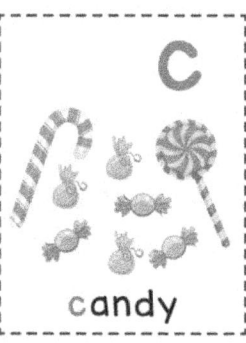 

g — grapes   o — octopus   c — candy   k — kite

. c

. o

. k

. g

Phonics Phase 2
i, n, m, t

match the picture with
the correct phonic

igloo

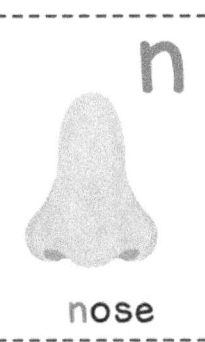
nose

mouse

dog

• i

• m

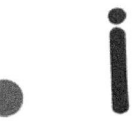

• n

• d

Phonics Phase 2
h, b, f, ff

match the picture with the correct phonic

h
heart

b
balloons

f
frog

ff
blast off

. b

. f

. h

. ff

Phonics Phase 2
ck, e, u, r
match the picture with the correct phonic

ck	e	u	r
 blocks	 eggplant	 umbrella	 robot

.ck

.r

.e

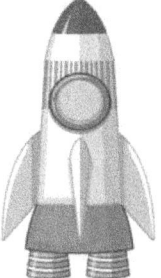

.u

Sight words

Color the word.

and

Trace the word.

and

Find and circle the word.

And how old are you?
She runs and he does too.
Cats and dogs are pets.

ant   and
can   ball
   man   land
and   art   and

Connect the letters.

p n e
a z d

Write the word.

Write the word in a sentence.

You _____ I are kids.

/ Sight words

Color the word.

are

Trace the word.

are

Find and circle the word.

We are family.
Are we there yet?
They are my dogs.

have   are
are   far
    are   can
bare   arm   are

Connect the letters.

d r i
a s e

Write the word.

Write the word in a sentence.

We _____ friends.

Sight words

Color the word.

be

Trace the word.

be

Find and circle the word.

Will you be my friend?
She can be kind.
Can I be in the middle?

can be
be   she
    bed   bee
the be   be

Connect the letters.

s e
b t

Write the word.

Write the word in a sentence.

I will _____ there.

Sight words

Color the word.

can

Trace the word.

can

Find and circle the word.

I can read.
Can you tell me a story?
Cats can be funny.

van can
can   to
    can   cat
cake man can

Connect the letters.

c z n
p a y

Write the word.

Write the word in a sentence.

I _____ do this!

Sight words

Color the word.

do

Trace the word.

do

Find and circle the word.

We do the dishes.
What can I do for you?
Do your dogs bark?

do   pot
doll   do
    boat
to   deer
    do   do

Connect the letters.

r o
d w

Write the word.

Write the word in a sentence.

We _____ our best.

Sight words

Color the word.
go

Trace the word.
go

Find and circle the word.

We will go to bed.
Let's go to John.
Can I go now?

off　　　go
go　　　　　　goat
　　　go
jug　　　　　　　　go
　　go　　　got

Connect the letters.
t o
g m

Write the word.

Write the word in a sentence.

I will _____ outside.

Sight words

Color the word.

see

Trace the word.

see

Find and circle the word.

Can you see me?
I am very smart, you see.
We can see the sun.

she   test
see   see
     seek
rest   see
   see   bee

Connect the letters.

g e l
s i e

Write the word.

Write the word in a sentence.

I _____ the moon.

Sight words

Color the word.

to

Trace the word.

to

Find and circle the word.

She walks to school.
Can I go to Grandma's house?
We are going to the beach.

her to toy
boat to
to of to elf

Connect the letters.

t f
v o

Write the word.

Write the word in a sentence.

Let's go _____ bed.

Sight words

Color the word.

the

Trace the word.

the

Find and circle the word.

I see the dog outside.
The cake smells good.
Where is the bus going?

the   she
beth   the
        heat   the
he   they   the

Connect the letters.

t s e
r h i

Write the word.

Write the word in a sentence.

I play with _____ toys.

Sight words

Color the word.

we

Trace the word.

we

Find and circle the word.

We can go cook now.
What will we eat?
We are on the same team.

me   we
we   when
      we   elk
he   water
   we

Connect the letters.

q e
w k

Write the word.

Write the word in a sentence.

Where will _____ go?

MANDALA
for kids

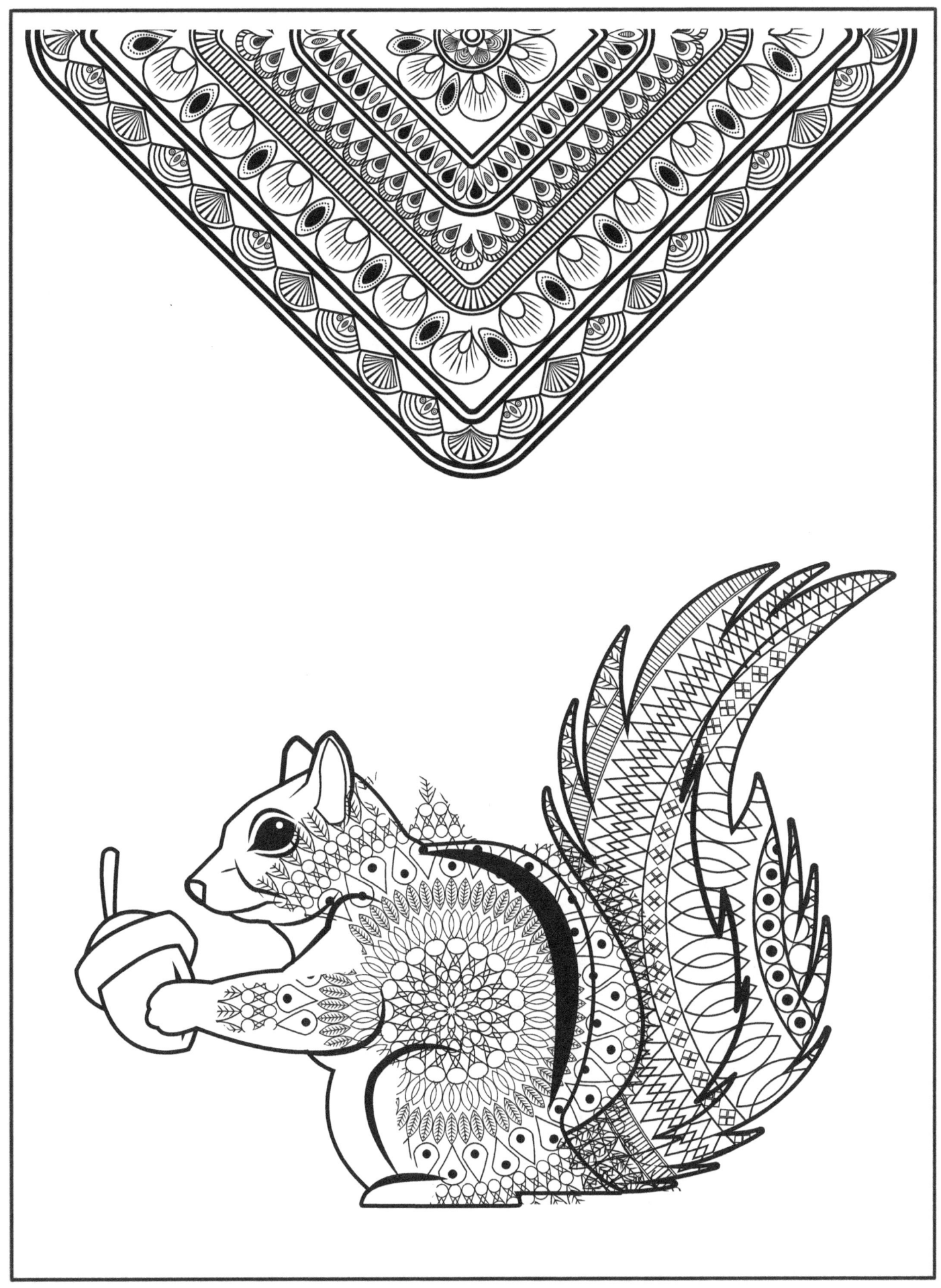

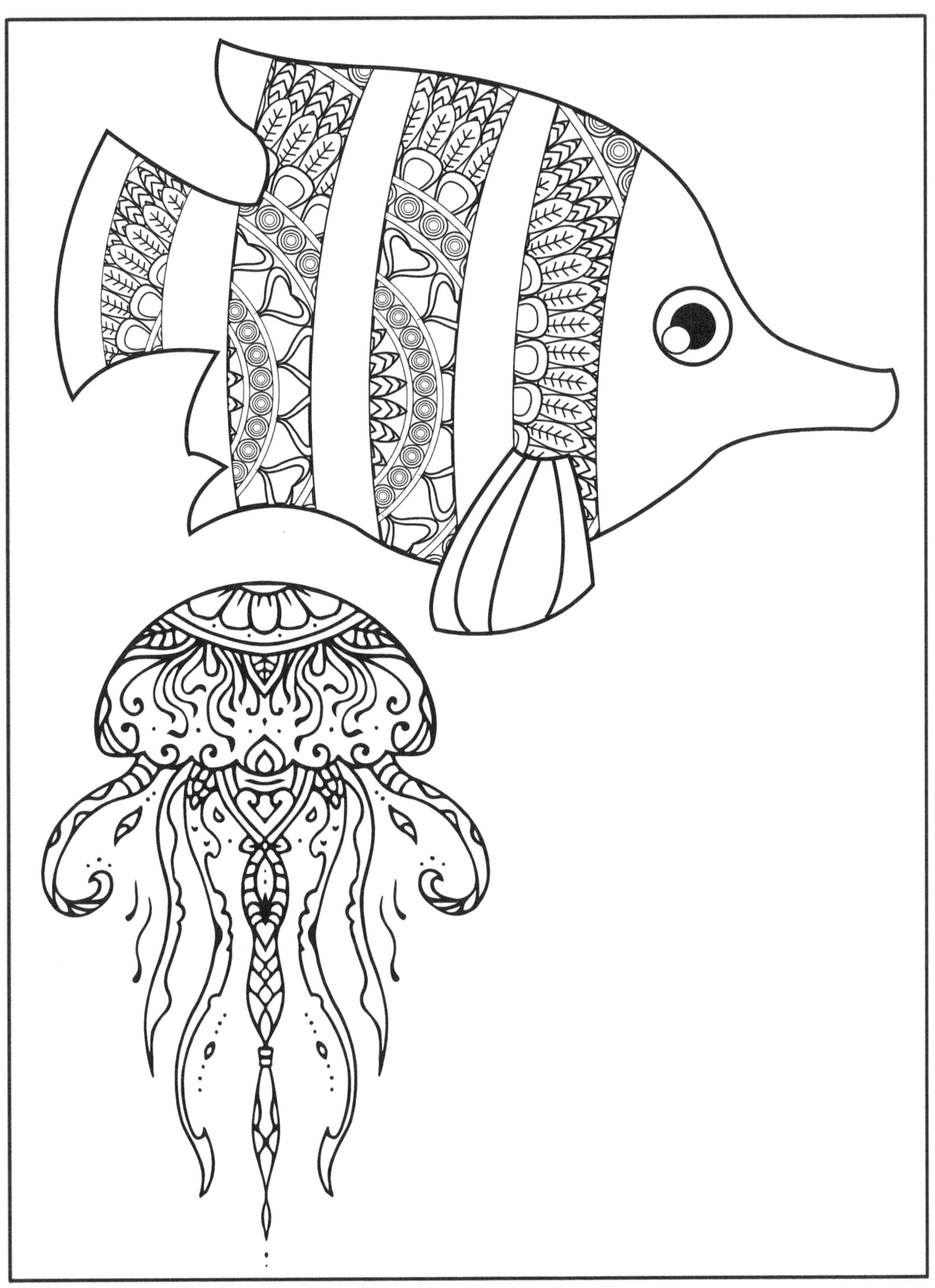

Thank you for choosing this book!

I hope your child enjoyed the activities in this book, as much we enjoyed creating it.
We are a small family business, so your feedback is very important to us.
If you have encountered any issues with your book, such as printing errors, faulty binding, paper bleeding or any other issue, please do not hesitate to contact us at:

 https://www.facebook.com/LittleEzraPublishing

 littleezra.publishing@gmail.com

Reviews are a brilliant thing for small businesses to grow and improve their quality, so if you enjoyed this book, please consider leaving a review on the website, adding photos of the interior and cover of this book. It takes few minutes, but it would be highly appreciated.

Thank you again for choosing us!

www.ingramcontent.com/pod-product-compliance
Lightning Source LLC
LaVergne TN
LVHW060202080526
838202LV00052B/4186